We'll Paint the Octopus Red

the Octopus Red

Stephanie Stuve-Bodeen
Illustrations by Pam DeVito

Woodbine House   1998

Library of Congress Cataloging-in-Publication Data

Stuve-Bodeen, Stephanie, 1965-
    We'll paint the octopus red / by Stephanie Stuve-Bodeen :
illustrated by Pam DeVito. -- 1st ed.
            p. cm.
    Summary: Emma and her father discuss what they will do when the
new baby arrives, but they adjust their expectations when he is born
with Down syndrome.
    ISBN-13: 978-1-890627-06-5 (hardcover)
    ISBN-10: 1-890627-06-2 (hardcover)
    [1. Down syndrome--Fiction.   2. Mentally handicapped--Fiction.
3. Brothers and sisters--Fiction.]   I. DeVito, Pam, ill.
II. Title.
PZ8.S94156Wg   1998
[E]--dc21

98-20591
CIP
AC

Printed in China, Shanghai(October 2019)

First edition
20 19 18

To Grandma Tiny, the writer, and Grandma Stuve, the reader.
Thanks for paving the way. – S.S.B.

For Jane Weinberger, with great affection. – P.D.

This morning my dad woke me up and told me I had a new baby brother named Isaac.

When my mom first told me I was getting a new
brother or sister, I wasn't very happy. I've had Mom
and Dad to myself for almost six years, and I like it that
way. Then I had a talk with Dad about all the things I
could do with my new brother or sister.

My dad said that when the baby is little, I can help change the diapers.
"That sounds yucky," I said.

My dad said that when the baby learns to sit up, I can roll a ball to it. "That sounds boring," I said.

My dad said that I can read books to the baby.
"I don't know how to read yet," I said.

My dad said that when the baby
gets bigger, we can play kickball
in the back yard.

"I bet I'll kick the ball
farther," I said.

Then I thought of some things all by myself. "When we go to Grandpa's farm, the baby can help me feed the calves with the nipple bottle." My dad said the baby could do that when it gets bigger.

"When we go for a ride in the mini-van, we can sit in the back and eat fruit snacks and stick out our tongues at cars that go by."

My dad said that the fruit snacks were okay, but he didn't think we should stick out our tongues.

"When we go downtown to the art festival, I can show the baby how to paint a picture with an octopus."

My dad said that sounded weird, but I explained that the octopus is only rubber, and you brush the paint on and then put the octopus on the paper. My dad made a face, but said that the baby would probably like that when it was older.

"When we go to see Aunt Wendy, the baby can go on the airplane with us. And I'll tell the baby to be really nice to Aunt Wendy, because she gives great presents."

My dad said the baby would definitely go on the plane with us, but that I should be nice to everyone, even if they don't give me presents.

"And someday, when we're both older, we'll go to Africa on a safari and see elephants and rhinos."

My dad said that we could go, but only if we took him along.

By the time we were done talking,
we'd thought of at least a million
things my new brother or
sister could do with me,
and I was ready to be a big sister.

But this morning, my dad's eyes were red when he woke me up. He said, "Emma, there's something you need to know about the baby." Then he said that Isaac had been born with something called Down syndrome. I guessed I knew what that meant. "Isaac won't be able to play kickball with me."

My dad said that Isaac might not walk as soon as other kids,
but he could probably learn to kick the ball when he's older.

"Isaac won't be able to feed the calves with a nipple bottle."
My dad said that Isaac might need some help, but he'd be able to do that too.

"He won't be able to ride in the back of the mini-van and eat fruit snacks and stick out his tongue at cars."

My dad smiled and said that he figured Isaac would be very good at both things.

"Then he won't be
able to paint the octopus."
    My dad said that he was positive
Isaac could do that if I showed him how.

"Will we take him along to
Aunt Wendy's?"
        My dad said we wouldn't go
without Isaac.

I knew the bad news was coming. "He won't be able to go with me on safari in Africa, will he?"

My dad said that he couldn't think of a reason why Isaac couldn't go.

By the time we were done talking, we couldn't find one of those million things that Isaac wouldn't be able to do with me. "If Isaac has this Down thing, then what can't he do?"

My dad hugged me. He said that as long as we were patient with Isaac, and helped him when he needed it, there probably wasn't anything he couldn't do.

We went to the hospital, and my mom was holding Isaac. I held his little hand. "Hi, Isaac. I'm your big sister, Emma." He smelled like baby powder when I leaned close to whisper in his ear, "I'll show you how to paint the octopus, Isaac, and I think we'll paint it red."

Questions & Answers about Down Syndrome

What is Down syndrome?

Down syndrome is something that causes differences in the way a baby looks and learns. No two babies with Down syndrome are quite the same, but they are often extra flexible, have eyes that slant upward, have small ears and a small nose, and grow more slowly than other kids. They also tend to learn more slowly than other babies. But every baby has his own personality and will look like other members of his family.

Why do some babies have Down syndrome?

Babies with Down syndrome are born with one extra chromosome in some or all of their cells. Chromosomes are tiny, thread-shaped things inside your body. They contain the directions that tell your body how to grow. These directions tell your body what color your eyes and hair will be, how big your nose will be, whether you will be a good singer, and many other things. When a baby has an extra chromosome, it mixes up his body's directions a little. That is why babies with Down syndrome look a little different from other babies and have to try harder to learn.

Nobody knows why some babies are born with Down syndrome, but we do know that it is nobody's fault.

Will the baby always have Down syndrome?

Yes. It is not something he will grow out of.

Why is it called Down syndrome?

A doctor named John Langdon Down was the first to write about this condition. He did not know all the things we know today about Down syndrome, but it is still named after him.

Can anyone catch Down syndrome from the baby?

No. The only way to get Down syndrome is to be born with it.

Why are some grown-ups sad when they hear the baby has Down syndrome?

Grown-ups might be sad because they did not plan to have a baby with Down syndrome. Sometimes they are worried because the baby might need to spend extra time at the hospital, or have to go back for an operation later. Grown-ups can also be scared if they don't know what to expect for their baby. It usually takes a little time for them to get used to their baby having Down syndrome, and then they can stop being sad and scared and just enjoy their new baby.

Why does the baby take up so much of Mom's and Dad's time?

All babies need lots of care because they cannot do anything for themselves at first. A baby with Down syndrome might need extra care because he might take longer to learn to do things like drink from a bottle or sit up. Mom and Dad may need to spend time teaching the baby to do things that other babies learn to do themselves. Sometimes brothers and sisters can help the baby learn, too.

Will the baby be able to talk when he's bigger?

Like any baby, he will understand what words mean before he can say them himself. If he has trouble learning to talk, he might be taught to make signs with his hands to tell people what he wants. When he is older, he will learn to talk, but he may not speak as clearly as other children. Brothers, sisters, and friends usually have no trouble understanding kids with Down syndrome.

Will the baby go to school just like any other kid when he gets older?

All children with Down syndrome go to school. Many go to the same school as their brothers or sisters, and some go to schools with special classes. Most children with Down syndrome learn how to read, write, do math problems, draw, play sports, and do the same things the other kids at school do. It just may take them longer to learn.

Why do people say that the baby is special?

Sometimes people say that babies with Down syndrome are special because they need extra time and help to learn. But they are also special in the same ways that other kids are special. All kids, with or without Down syndrome, are special because they have their own interests, talents, and personalities. If you take the time to get to know any child, you will discover that he is special in his own way.

Woodbine House would like to thank the many parents who contributed questions to be answered in this section. These are questions that children in their families have asked about their brother or sister with Down syndrome.